Journey Into More
God's Invitation

By Sandi Sadako

ISBN: 979-8-9856562-0-6

Edited by: Krista Dunk
Cover design by Romana Bovan

Dedication

I dedicate this book to:

Holy Spirit

You took me on an unfolding journey of faith,
despite the discomfort and unfamiliarity.
You taught me how to bypass my analytical mind
that wanted to overthink Your promptings.

You showed me that when You lead me to pray for people,
they feel the love of God.
Thank You for letting me discover more of who You are
at a pace that makes me want more.

Table of Contents

Foreword

Not many people would be able to understand what it's like to embark on a three-month outreach across the U.S. and Canada with a music and missions organization. This on a 35-foot bus with 20 team members, performing concerts every evening and staying in a different host home each night. And – here's the kicker – all the while caring for your nursing baby. Not many, indeed! But Sandi does.

My Erin and her Matthew were under six months of age when Sandi and I, and our husbands, began that ministry tour. But it was during those three months that a very close, very precious friendship began. Now almost 30 years later, we have journeyed together through many seasons of life, from raising toddlers to homeschooling children to helping our grown kids launch into adulthood. Through it all, our friendship has morphed and strengthened, expanding in ways neither of us could have known or guessed we needed from those early days on the bus. But our Heavenly Father knew. And I am forever grateful.

In the last three years especially, our friendship has taken an even deeper dive into a level of trust and connection that we hadn't yet experienced. Hours upon hours of rich weekly prayer times and vulnerable conversations have forged an iron-sharpens-iron relationship. Sharing about the tender heart of our Father for us, about fresh profound discoveries from our times in the Word, and breath-taking Spirit-led adventures into risk and trust...our hearts have been fused and enriched with an eternal bond.

Through these years, I've watched Sandi's heart become more

and more deeply rooted and firmly grounded in the love of God for her as she's plumbed the width and length and height and depth of it. Her journey has inspired, challenged, encouraged, healed, and emboldened my own journey. It's been an adventure of joy and delight and wonder.

The words she has penned on the following pages flow from that place of personal expedition. They are powerful and transformative because they are coming from her years of walking hand in hand with her precious Savior, tuning her ear to the voice of His Spirit and receiving, again and again, the un-ending affection and unearned favor of her Heavenly Father – the One who calls her His beloved.

I invite you to feast on the words she writes, the scriptures she treasures and the stories she shares. I believe that you, like me, will be changed and delighted by time spent with her.

Jill Ludlow
Co-Founder, Full Sail Ministries

Introduction

Growing up in a church that only acknowledged the Holy Spirit when reciting the Apostle's Creed left me with a faith that believed God lived somewhere up in the clouds, separate from my daily life. I was to live down here on earth and look forward to seeing Him at the end of my life. There were no sermons about hearing God's voice. There were no teachings about the gifts of the Holy Spirit. I mostly learned about God, Jesus and giving to good causes.

I recall having an excellent fifth-grade Sunday school teacher who inspired me to memorize the books of the Bible. Admittingly, my Sunday school teacher gave points for various activities like memorization, and my competitive nature drove me to earn as many points as possible. It wasn't until my college years when this familiarity with the books of the Bible came in handy.

In my early twenties, moving to my first missionary assignment in another state, I encountered the reality of the Holy Spirit as a power source for living and a catalyst for direction, insight and clarity. "And you shall receive power when the Holy Spirit comes upon you, and you shall be My witnesses in Jerusalem, and in all Judea and Samaria and even to the remotest part of the earth." Acts 1:8

Decades later, increased awareness of who Holy Spirit is sent me on a journey to learn more. The first three chapters of this book talk about this growth phase. The momentum continued to grow, and with it, a sense of anticipation of the *more* that God had for me.

In reading my January 2020 journal, there was a sense of expectation, a knowing that there was more to my relationship with God.

> "I feel like I'm on the cusp of realizing a nugget of wisdom, the key, to knowing You intimately. Meeting with You in the hidden places seems to be a piece to that. But I don't know where those places exist."

Several months later, God led me to Psalm 25:14 TPT:

"There is a private place reserved for the lovers of God when they sit near Him and receive the revelation secrets of His promises."

The simplicity of learning to sit near Him became my reality. I learned to linger with God before charging into my day. Some of the things He revealed to me might be new for you, as they were to me at the time. As I said, I come from a conservative background. Yet, His undeniable love led me through every situation I share in these chapters. Allow Holy Spirit to speak to your spirit in gentle whispers as you consider the journey you're about to take.

In some places, I've referred to the Holy Spirit or the Father without the article, "the." This reflects where I was in my journey at the time of the writing. I had the option to make all the designations consistent throughout, but I wanted you to get a feel of the various stages of my journey. The chapters after the first three are not in chronological order, so you will sometimes see "the" when I refer to Holy Spirit and Father. Now, I mostly say Father and Holy Spirit because of the intimacy I am experiencing.

Several conversations between Father and me were captured

in my journals and shared in this book. For easier reading, I've indented and put the portions of the conversation that God spoke in italics.

When you see parenthesis around a scripture reference, I'm letting you know the verse where part of the previous sentence came from.

One more thing: when I asked Father what His heart is for you, the reader, out poured this love letter titled, "The Invitation." You will want to read this before diving into the chapters, because it is written to you. God had you in mind long before you picked up this book.

Thank you for going on this journey with me. Are you ready? He is waiting for you!

God's Invitation

My Beloved,

You are my very heart. I love you with an everlasting love. You make me smile as I see you go about your day. I understand that you have unvoiced questions about your life, the people in your world, your future, your past, and about Me. I long to hear your voice. Will you bring Me into those things that are close to your heart?

It's one thing to keep your hands busy, so you do not have to think about those consuming thoughts. Distraction has its place. Let Me show you another way.

My heart is for you. My intentions are good toward you. My presence surrounds you. You are hidden with Christ in Me.

As you linger with Me, I will show you many things. Would you like to hear My voice more clearly? Come, sit with Me. Ask Me anything. If I don't tell you, it's because I want you to journey with Me in discovering the answer. Do you trust Me to lead you? I am the Good Shepherd. I have great experience in leading My flock. When one strays, I go after it and bring it back into My care. Every one of My sheep is valuable to Me, and I love them. They trust Me and respond to My voice.

Some sheep hear My voice more clearly than others. The ones on the edges have their eyes on things outside the perimeter and have selective hearing. The ones who remain closest to Me immediately respond to my voice. These are eager for connection with Me.

I tenderly care for every one of My sheep, and I enjoy being with them. Come, sit with Me.

Love,

Your Good Shepherd

Section One
God's Compassion

Chapter One:

Starting Point

Journeying into the *more* of God began with an unexpected Facebook message from a missionary friend I met in Japan who now lives in Hungary. We hadn't seen each other in nearly three decades but remained close through letters and occasional phone calls. She and her husband didn't know about my desire to plan a milestone birthday trip, but they invited me to come for a visit. They offered to feed and house me. All I had to provide was a plane ticket to their home in Budapest. I had no idea this trip would catapult me into more than I could have ever imagined.

Baggage claim at the Budapest airport took longer than expected, but moving through the exit doors, I spotted my petite, blond-haired friend. We hugged and talked non-stop as she showed me the sights of her city. After a few days of seeing typical tourist locations, I looked forward to getting to see snippets of her day-to-day life.

She took me to two different grocery stores, one near her home and another near the place her daughter took piano lessons. What were errands to her were grand adventures for me. Grocery stores are great places to pick up souvenir items to take back to my foodie family. That day, I picked up cookies and paprika.

Walking and talking in two different parks gave me a glimpse into places that provided a respite from city life. One had Beethoven's home set against the backdrop of tall trees with a lake in the foreground. It was relaxing to walk around that park.

The sights and sounds of this trip were a welcomed relief from six months of challenging ministry transition. Even though God prompted the change in my assignment, which involved less administrative service and more intercessory prayer, it wasn't an easy change.

Halfway through my stay in Budapest, my friend and I woke up early, caught the train and headed to a place I'd never been: Vienna, Austria. I didn't know God was up to something. I had simply made a choice between visiting Prague or Vienna. While watching the European scenery speed by as I sat next to my friend, something unexpected happened.

The warmth of God's love filled my entire being when I recounted the events that took place to get me in that window seat. Not only did He provide me with an unexpected trip, but also, I was adventuring with my friend whom I'd known for 31 years. I had tried to plan other trips for my milestone birthday, such as a cruise with a long-time friend, a trip to visit Hawaii friends or a visit to Alaska, but they hadn't worked out. Instead, God gifted me with this experience that included having enough reward miles for a free plane ticket, and I felt loved.

With rattling train tracks beneath my feet, God and I shared something imperceptible to the people in that train car. The realization hit me. God invited me into His unconditional love, and I only needed to receive. His love was on display on a whole new level. He saw me, wanted to bless me and pre-arranged this celebratory trip. In response, my eyes welled up with tears as I realized His genuine affection for me.

He set me up to experience His lavish love when I least expected it!

I couldn't help but entrust every area of my life to Him. I wasn't knowingly holding anything back; it was more of a deeper surrender of my entire being. Because He led me to experience this deep love, I knew I could trust Him with everything. Even with the unknowns of my future involvement in a ministry I believed in, I trusted Him. God's unconditional love brought me to absolute surrender. I felt securely wrapped in His love.

As if the Budapest trip wasn't enough, God further poured out His love by having one of my return flight layovers be in Tokyo, Japan. While having a meal in the Tokyo airport, memories of doing campus ministry alongside my Budapest friend flooded my mind. Even though it was the middle of the night when we got back on the plane, I didn't sleep. Instead, I processed this experience with gratitude, writing page after page in my journal while most other passengers slept.

At one point, the pilot announced we were flying over the Colorado Rocky Mountains. My heart leapt. Our friendship (my friend who I'd said goodbye to at the Budapest airport) started in Japan and included visits to Colorado and California. By seeing or experiencing all four locations where our 31-year-old friendship grew, it seemed as if God put an exclamation mark on His incredible act of love. This was way beyond anything I could've planned. Only God!

Upon returning to California, I noticed something different about myself. I felt more tender toward the people around me. Instead of walking into the grocery store with shopping list in hand and blinders on to anything that slowed me down, I shopped with a different heart posture. I was open to Holy Spirit drawing my attention to people in need of healing, an encouraging word or a smile. God's love filled my heart to overflowing, and it spilled out onto people nearby. The valve had opened, and love overflowed.

In daily life, God empowered me to do things I didn't normally do. I'm an introvert, and the things I saw God do in and through me were beyond my natural capacity. Something inside me changed. That day on the train to Vienna changed my life. God opened doors, and I said yes to walking through them.

One night, after a prayer meeting, I did something uncharacteristic. Needing to get my purse and car keys, I tiptoed back into my friend's living room, where the prayer meeting had just ended. One of the three people on the couch was praying. Instead of heading toward the door, I waited for a pause, then prayed the words God put on my heart for this person.

Typically, I would've quietly gathered my belongings and moved toward the front door. That night, I got invited to partner with God in what He was doing. I did not know what they had been praying, but I prayed with them as Holy Spirit led. Later, I learned from my friend that the words I prayed made sense and fit into the context of their prayers. That was new. Thank you, Lord!

This truth from Romans was the catalyst to this unusual behavior:

"...and hope does not disappoint, because the love of God has been poured out within our hearts through the Holy Spirit who was given to us." Romans 5:5

I continued to see increasing boldness and love flow out of me, not only in my city, but when I visited friends in their towns.

Once in downtown Indianapolis, my friend and I looked for a coffee place in a food vendor area. Most were closed because it was late in the afternoon. As we turned down the last aisle, we found one coffee stand still open. We placed our order with the lone employee and stood back from the counter. While waiting for our coffees, something familiar happened. I knew God wanted me to pray for the barista.

When the burly barista turned to hand us our coffees, I looked him in the eyes, told him that God wanted to bless his business and asked if I could pray. He nodded in assent and leaned forward with one elbow resting on the counter as I prayed. Linda bowed her head in agreement.

After the "amen," the barista asked in a deep voice, "What made you pray for me?" Without hesitation, I told him how God had prompted me to pray because He wanted to bless his business. The barista responded, "I'm a pastor." He then told us stories from his overseas mission trips. He testified that people had dreams about Jesus then were drawn toward churches shortly after. Their dreams led them into a relationship with Jesus.

The barista's testimonies and the Holy Spirit leading me to pray encouraged my friend. I had told Linda about experiencing the *more* of God and how my life had changed. That day, she saw for herself how the love of God flowed through me to encourage a random barista who happened to be a pastor.

One thing I've noticed about God is how He shows love in ways we each can understand. How He communicates love to me is probably different from how He shows love to you. For me, the culmination of details getting me on that train to Vienna was evidence of God's unconditional love. The entire Budapest trip was an unforgettable birthday adventure. His warm affection and inviting presence led me to the place of full surrender, holding nothing back from Him. This became my starting point into more.

"We love because He first loved us." 1 John 4:19

Chapter Two:

Quest For More

Returning from a spontaneous trip to visit a friend in Hawaii, I felt different. My friend showed me two documentaries with evidence of the Holy Spirit in action, and I had never seen anything like it. Testimony after testimony showed God's healing power in the captivating scenes. As a result, I wondered, "Could I learn to follow Holy Spirit's leading like that?" Most of what I saw in the documentaries were not situations I'd ever seen, even though I had done missionary work in over a dozen countries and 49 states.

Although I had my prayer language, the incidences I watched onscreen at my friend's house made me realize how little I knew about Holy Spirit. I observed how operating in the supernatural wasn't a formula or a checklist. Love seemed to be the key to encountering the Holy Spirit. My curiosity and wonder increased, and I wanted more. My new adventure and prayer became:

"Holy Spirit, who are You? I want to learn more."

On my first day back home from Hawaii, I received a reminder: the women's conference at my church started that evening. I had forgotten about it but remembered why I bought the ticket. Identity in Christ, one of my favorite topics, was the event's theme. In my early twenties, a greater understanding of who I am in Christ built a solid foundation of faith. It was my experience that I needed to shore up my identity in various unfolding life phases.

That evening during the opening worship time, I heard God clearly say to me:

"I launch you into ministry."

I continued worshipping, not truly understanding the meaning of the words. The rest of the conference was good, but that phrase during the opening night was my biggest takeaway.

A few days after the conference, I decided to get back to the gym. It became clear that even my routine activities were changing. Little did I know the fitness center would become a training ground, not only for my body but my faith as well.

Exiting through the waist-high gate after a vigorous workout, I saw a friend I hadn't seen in years. She stood to the right of the front door, watching people go in and out of the lobby, not seeming to mind the background noise of weight machines clanking and treadmills running. While saying hello and starting a conversation, I suddenly felt the Holy Spirit nudge me to pray for her.

My friend used to be on the prayer team at church, so I knew she'd say yes to me praying for her. Ideally, I wanted to move away from the front door traffic and go to a table at the gym café about ten feet away. Instead, my friend bowed her head right where she stood and waited for me to start praying. So much for my ideal scenario of being inconspicuous.

I prayed for her near the steady stream of people coming and going. I felt exposed and closed my eyes to block out everyone walking past us. It was all I could do to focus on praying and ignore the awkwardness of our location. This situation felt like it was more for my training to say "yes" to God's invitation to pray than a blessing to my friend.

Another awkward experience of praying for someone in public happened at a restaurant with a friend. The meal ended, and my friend sat on the other side of the table. I knew I was supposed to pray for her. How did I know? The thought dropped into my brain. I didn't generate it.

She was a missionary friend, so I knew she'd say yes too. Rejection wasn't the problem; the problem was the location of our table. We were in the center of the dining area, and the lunch crowd filled every table. Once again, I felt conspicuous. This time I kept my eyes open while praying but was a bit distracted. I can't say it was a powerful prayer, but I was obedient to the Holy Spirit's prompting.

It wasn't long before I understood what had happened to me in Hawaii. Before I left the island, I felt a stirring in my heart and said silently, "I thought I knew You. Who are You, Holy Spirit?"

My capacity increased in my quest to learn more about the Holy Spirit. I felt a renewed love for people as I went out into the community. It felt like a new measure of God's love had been poured out in my heart through the Holy Spirit (Romans 5:5). I walked expectantly into stores, silently asking God, "Is there someone here who You want me to pray for?"

Here is what happened when I visited a store in the nearby outlet mall. One of the workers behind the counter, who was unpacking a box of clothing, drew my attention. I asked if she had allergies. She said they were pretty bad, so I offered to pray for her. Although surprised, she agreed, and I prayed. Her boss, who was standing nearby, didn't seem to mind; in fact, she had a knowing smile on her face after I said, "Amen."

At a local grocery store, a cashier suffered from back pain. I sometimes felt hesitant to pray in stores when people were waiting in line behind me – not because I was self-conscious, but because I didn't want to cause delay for the people waiting in line.

One day at this grocery store, I went through one of the four self-checkout stands. There she was: the cashier with back pain was nearby. Since there were no other customers around, I asked if I could pray for her back, and she said, "Yes!" I immediately placed my hand on her lower back. The prayer that came out was short, but it didn't matter; God healed her!

Several weeks later, when I went through her checkout stand, she testified to the woman bagging my groceries, "This is the lady who prayed for my back, and God healed it!" The clerk who was bagging the groceries asked which church I attended. When I said the name, the cashier exclaimed that she attended the same church. Because our church had four services, we hadn't seen each other. We were both thankful our paths had crossed at her grocery store.

Speaking of church, once, a lady sat in the row in front of me, and the Holy Spirit let me know she had back pain. I knew I was supposed to pray for her; the question was, "When, Lord?" I didn't want to interrupt her time of worship, nor did I want to wait until the end of service and risk her leaving before getting prayer. I silently prayed, "Let me know when I'm supposed to pray for her," and I kept worshipping.

A few minutes later, as the worship song drew to a close, I saw the word "Now!" in my mind. Without overthinking it, I leaned over and asked the lady if I could pray for her back pain. She looked at me with astonishment as if to say, "How did you know?" With a nod of her head, she said, "Yes." As she closed her eyes, I put my hand on her back and prayed for healing. The worship team was in the middle of singing "Good, Good Father" by the time I said, "Amen!"

Not wanting to disturb the people around us, we didn't have any follow-up conversation. I continued in worship, not knowing if her back felt better. At the end of service, our pastor felt compelled to ask the ones who needed healing for back pain to stand. The lady in front of me turned around to look at me and declared, "I'm already healed!"

With opportunities to pray for people showing up all over town, I realized praying for people was worth the occasional discomfort. Being obedient to Holy Spirit's promptings overrode needing to be eloquent or set in the ideal environment. No matter the outcome of the prayer, people felt seen and loved by God. That's always a win.

Sometimes instead of an idea in my mind, my body will cue me when it's time to pray for the person in front of me. This reaction happened in an online breakout room as a woman talked about her life. A tingling sensation pulsed through my body, and I got fidgety. After the gal finished, I asked if I could pray, and she eagerly said, "Yes." She was in tears and said afterward, "Thank you so much for your prayers today. I can't tell you how much I needed every word you spoke."

It was the love of God poured into my heart through the Holy Spirit (Romans 5:5) that prompted each of these interactions. Without this, I would've felt too self-conscious to reach out. Now, I feel eager anticipation when I pray for people because it's an invitation to let the love of God flow through me. I get to step into situations that God has already prepared beforehand.

"For we are His workmanship, created in Christ Jesus for good works, which God prepared beforehand so that we would walk in them." Ephesians 2:10

Chapter Three:

Embrace

Being raised with the belief that it was best not to make waves, my behavior out in public felt strange. The Japanese phrase playing through my mind was, "The nail that sticks up gets hammered down." My actions of praying for people whenever I felt prompted by Holy Spirit were out of character, but I didn't mind. Prayer opportunities were often happening, and my expectation of God showing off His goodness enlarged.

Driving around town doing errands one day, I got to thinking about how love had grown in my life as I learned about Holy Spirit. My curiosity prompted me to pray, "How can I love well?" The answer came, "Love the one you're with." I understood that to mean being fully present and engaged with the person in front of me.

A few days later, another question popped up in my prayers. This one had to do with limitless faith. In a self-reflective journal exercise, I asked myself, "Why do I want limitless faith?"

"So, I can experience all You have for me.

So, I can be all You want me to be.

So, I don't limit Your intended design for me.

I want to experience so much of Your love that I can't help but love You and
love the people around me. These reasons sound like relationship, loving and believing I'm loved.

I want limitless faith, not for what I can do, but for a deeper relationship with You, Father, and a better connection with people. Christ in me, the hope of glory (Colossians 1:27), causes me to realize how much of me is unexplored. I mean, granted, since my 2014 Budapest and Hawaii trips, conquered territory, shifted mindsets happened, but I believe there is so much more."

Shortly after writing this journal entry, the realization hit me that Jesus had always been my abiding place or the main focus in my life as a believer. Being approachable and friendly, Jesus was my go-to for friendship. The One whom I had difficulty expressing affection for was Father God. Although I had committed Hebrews 4:16, to memory, "Therefore let us draw near with confidence to the throne of grace, so that we may receive mercy and find grace to help in time of need," I still did not feel comfortable getting close to Him. Being confident that I *can* approach Father God didn't necessarily mean I felt courageous to do so.

After recognizing my hesitancy to be with Father God, this thought came to mind, "Jesus feels comfortable with His Father!" Jesus had always felt safe to me, and He is who I comfortably approached day-to-day. I decided to ask Jesus to walk me over to Father God, knowing He would lead me in safety.

As I sat still, closed my eyes and waited, I felt as if Jesus took my hand, and together we walked toward Father. As soon as we got near Him, Jesus released my hand and gave me an encouraging nod with a twinkle in His eyes to signal that everything was fine. After taking the last few steps on my own, I plopped myself down. At first, I sat awkwardly beside Father because I didn't feel comfortable facing Him.

Once I grew accustomed to being next to Him, which took several weeks, I did a random thing as He stood up. I pictured myself as a child standing in front of my Father. Without thinking, I reached up, fingers intertwined and locked together behind His neck, while my legs dangled off the ground in anticipation of swinging in circles. I giggled when Father playfully turned around and around, slowly at first, then faster as I squealed, "Faster! Faster!" My heart warmed and my defenses lowered as we laughed and played together.

Even though laughing together helped me feel more comfortable, a part of me still felt wary being this close to Father. What He did next surprised me. He completely broke through my guardedness. It happened while watching a weekly dance show on TV. I was mesmerized by a female dancer who courageously glided across the dance floor despite losing her grandmother to Alzheimer's five days prior.

When the music ended, it was as if a dam burst, and the graceful dancer let her tears flow freely. Her professional dance partner gently pulled her close and embraced her while she openly wept. The strong, beautiful dancer no longer held in the pain of her loss as the protective arms of her dance partner let her know that she wasn't alone. His embrace gave her a safe place to express her sadness.

At that moment, I also wept. For the first time, I realized the heart of God, my Father. He longed for me to let Him place His arms around me and hold me close, be my resting place, my place of safety and security. He wanted me to let Him love me in a way no one else ever could. I finally understood He was safe, and I could trust Him.

In my mind's eye, I pictured myself crawling onto His lap, His arms encircled around me, with my head leaning against His chest. I felt safe and accepted. Letting go of my self-protective resistance hadn't left me feeling as exposed as I had anticipated. I belonged near the heart of Father, resting on His lap feeling seen, known and loved.

This revelation of Father's love drew me deeper into intimacy with Him. In some ways, I felt giddy with excitement at my newfound love. It wasn't new to Him, but His love, experienced in this way, was new to me. The love of God filled me in a way I hadn't known was missing from my life.

Since this encounter, Father's lap has been my favorite resting place. No longer does He feel unapproachable. I am not afraid of Him, nor do I feel the need to keep my guard up around Him. Sometimes I'll lean sideways on Him with my left ear pressed against his chest. I can't say that I hear His heartbeat, but being near Him like this feels anchoring and calming. Being near Him is my favorite place to be!

"Because I set you, Yahweh, always close to me, my confidence will never be weakened, for I experience your wraparound presence every moment." Psalm 16:8 TPT

Chapter Four:

Right Place, Right Time

During my second missionary trip to Thailand, God put me in an unexpected situation to unlock the truest version of myself. It had been 23 years since I gave a testimony utilizing a translator. And yet being out of practice is not a disqualifier from Kingdom work. The morning of our Thai Women's Conference, I sat with our worship leader among the rows of chairs in the church hosting our event. She asked if I'd share my Father's embrace story: my journey into becoming comfortable in Father's presence.

At first, I told her, "I don't know if I can get through it." My emotions were so raw and tears so close to the surface. The day before, as I walked around the outside of the church by myself praying for the Thai ladies, tears streamed down my face. I just wanted these ladies to get it – to understand and respond to the depth and richness of Father's love for them.

Amidst my feelings of uncertainty, these words came to mind: the enemy is defeated by the blood of the Lamb and the word of our testimony. The word of *my* testimony! This reminder from Revelation 12:11 gave me a surge of courage and willingness to share from that place of intimacy in my relationship with Father. This unanticipated opportunity was not about me.

I wrote in my journal:

"Suddenly, I am a WEAPON in Father's hand, not a liability or incompetent in the Kingdom."

Several team members prayed with me, and I prayed with my translator, whom I had met on a previous trip to Thailand. I was comforted to know that Carmen would be standing nearby communicating the message of Father's love in a way the women understood.

I asked my translator if the Thai women would understand when I talked about having a picture in my head of Jesus walking me over to Father, God. Her reply eased my concern. Carmen said they already had visions; my words would put good visions in their head.

The truth that I was a weapon, the prayers prayed over me and my team supporting me felt empowering and gave me the courage to step up to the mic that evening. At the beginning of the worship time, Holy Spirit gave me the idea to talk about how I felt in God's presence during worship. I'd not used this word before, but the word "clean" came to mind along with loved, known, cherished and safe.

Making my way to the platform, I segued out of "Here I Am to Worship" and launched into the story of how I grew in intimacy with Father. The words flowed, and I remembered to pause in between sentences to give my friend time to translate. And, wouldn't you know it, the part of my testimony that got the most significant reaction from the ladies was when I said the word, "clean." God knew it would resonate with them

Flowing in Holy Spirit's leading felt so easy and enjoyable! I looked into people's eyes and felt Father's love flowing through me. I relived the scenario of Jesus taking my hand and walking me to Father's side. I talked about my process of trusting

Father and letting Him wrap His arms around me, and it felt so right! Being that vulnerable, talking about my intimate moments with Father in a public setting was a breakthrough moment for me personally.

God had been chipping away at my analytical ability when praying for people back home. I noticed my logic caused me to overthink the Holy Spirit's promptings, which then led to questioning what I heard. It was easier to follow through on loving the one in front of me when I stopped being so analytical about it.

Another thing that defied my logic was how I'd see a green dot sticker, about an inch in diameter, on people's backs when Father wanted to heal them. All I had to do was place my hand where I saw the green dot, and their back got healed. Again, it was easy. All I had to do was partner with God in what He was already doing.

God took my analytical, information-gatherer strengths and let me practice Spirit-led living more profoundly than ever before. As I practiced, in often new and uncomfortable settings, my learning curve sped up. I was learning how to operate out of the deepest, most authentic part of me.

Half of our missionary team went back to the States after two women's conferences in Chiang Mai. The half I was with traveled to Chonburi, where we participated in our missionary friend's denominational conference. I got to be part of the team tasked with setting up a prayer room and being available to pray with and for the attendees. I enjoyed this week-long opportunity to see the people I prayed with during breaks and meals, allowing for further conversation.

Our first morning there, I woke up from a dream where God

told me that it only takes a moment to touch a person's heart. It could be through a look, a word, a speaker or any other element at this conference. There was no pressure on any one person to influence another. It's a privilege to be in the right place at the right time to be part of that person's process. I felt as if my spirit had been in prayer most of the early morning before waking.

Since it was a conference, we attended the sessions alongside the missionaries and pastors. During one main session at this denominational conference, I closed my eyes to pray. God gave me a picture of a woman wearing an all-white outfit, top and bottom. Then, He gave me a picture of what to pray for her. I knew I needed to find her after the session ended, even though I had no idea where she was sitting among the several hundred people in attendance.

God is faithful to carry to completion what He starts. I only had to look about two rows in front of me, and there sat a woman wearing a white denim jacket and a white skirt. As soon as the speaker finished, I made a beeline to the woman in white. She looked a bit surprised by my sudden appearance, but when I asked if I could pray for her, she relaxed and nodded.

The word that God put on my heart to pray was right on target. She was a pastor's wife, and God knew what she needed. The next day when I saw her at dinner, she told me the picture I had seen for her represented hope. She realized that He was working on her behalf, and she felt free! In response, I got to share another picture God had given me for her when I prayed that morning. It was a blessing to have run into her at dinner and delivered the second encouraging word.

Being in the right place at the right time on several occasions throughout my time in Thailand increased my faith and courage. Not only was it a privilege to pray with leaders from all over the world, but it was a blessing to have a conversation over meals. The unexpected opportunity to share my Father's embrace testimony at our Thai women's conference caused me to realize I am a weapon in God's hands. As a result, I returned to the U.S. a different person, on fire and ready for whatever journey God wanted to take me on next.

Chapter Five:

C'mon, Baby Girl

"I lift up my eyes to the mountains where does my help come from? My help comes from the LORD, the Maker of heaven and earth. He will not let your foot slip—He who watches over you will not slumber." Psalm 121:1-3a NIV

Several years ago, while experiencing growing pains as a beginning worship leader, Father encouraged me in a unique way. Sitting in His presence one morning, He gave me a picture of myself as a little girl trying to complete a daunting feat.

A dark forest with towering trees swallowed up my child-sized frame. Even though it was daytime, the dense treetops blocked the sunlight from hitting the ground. There were unfamiliar animal noises in the distance; insects all around.

My focus was navigating across a murky pond by carefully placing my feet on top of the slippery rocks. Progress was slow as I looked down at each stone, picking the ones that seemed the steadiest. With barely enough light to see the next step, it was hard to tell how much further I had to go.

Suddenly, a bit of movement across the pond caught my eye. There was an outline of a person intently watching me.

It was Jesus! He broke through my concentration and fear. With outstretched arms and a smile on His face, He cheered me on, saying, "C'mon, baby girl!" I locked eyes with His and bounded across the last half of the submerged rocks.

Leaping into His embrace, I felt joy, courage and confidence. He had been there all along, waiting and watching me struggle on my own. Once I shifted my eyes to meet His, I felt brave and able to complete the difficult task in front of me. His open arms were an invitation to safety.

What I realized through this encounter in the forest is that it's not necessary to struggle alone. Even though the algae-covered rocks drew my eyes downward, I needed to position my head to look up. Jesus continually gives the invitation, "C'mon, Baby Girl!" when navigating the messy, in-between times (those slippery rocks).

He is asking, *"Will you let Me take you from your pain point to your breakthrough?"*

The messy middle represents me trying to figure things out. I gather information, sort through the pieces of content and formulate questions. I'm an internal processor, and having a two-way conversation with God in writing helps uncover my buried thoughts and emotions. I feel safe tossing out questions, hoping they bring clarity. Sometimes God answers with a follow-up question; other times, He answers directly. It has the feel of warming up on the tennis court, hitting the ball back and forth.

This forest scenario encouraged me to look up when starting down a path of trying something new. This past year, *new* involved learning how to teach online workshops. The steep learning curve felt as if I'd grabbed the railing on the end of a high-speed train, body flying parallel to the tracks, holding on for dear life! New vocabulary and new technical skills came at me at an accelerated pace. While I enjoyed the teaching aspect and learning how to serve my online community, some of the design steps leading up to that part were daunting.

At times I felt exhilarated when implementing skills I hadn't known just months prior. Clicking a button on my newly created website and watching it take me to its intended page made me feel accomplished. Other times, I put one foot in front of the other toward unfamiliarity, implementing the training, walking forward in faith, trying not to feel overwhelmed.

Do you remember the Bible story of a man named Peter, who walked on water? At first, the disciples in the boat were scared, but look at the dialogue between Peter and Jesus.

Jesus: "*Take courage; it is I. Don't be afraid!*"

Peter: "Lord, if it's You, tell me to come to You on the water."

Jesus: "Come."

At first, Peter seemed up for the challenge and courageously jumped out of the boat. Once outside the familiarity of the fishing boat and walking on water, something happened. Matthew 14:30 says he became frightened and beginning to sink; he cried out, "Lord, save me!" Instead of keeping his gaze on Jesus, He looked at the thing causing the disturbance around him, the storm. The impact of the wind was more important than the wooing of Jesus' eyes.

When I'm feeling afraid or overwhelmed, I need to ask myself, "What am I looking at?" Am I looking at my circumstances, or am I looking at Jesus?"

Matthew 14:31 tells us what Jesus said to Peter when he began to sink, "You of little faith, why did you doubt?"

There is no record of Peter's response. I don't know if he felt exhilarated that he had walked on water, surprised that he was sinking, or embarrassed that Jesus had rescued him from drowning. After all, Peter was a fisherman, so that was not his first time in a boat or on the sea. I'm guessing it all happened so fast he did not have time to process the event.

Again, this simple question is powerful: "You of little faith, why did you doubt?" I wonder how Peter received those words from Jesus.

According to Matthew 14:32-33 TPT, we learn what happens next.

"And the very moment they both stepped into the boat, the raging wind ceased. Then all the disciples bowed down before him and worshiped Jesus. They said in adoration, 'You are truly the Son of God!'"

The operative word here is "all." All the disciples bowed down, which meant Peter also bowed down. They had a worship time in the boat! They all focused on Jesus!

Do my circumstances have to change before I focus on Jesus? It's so easy to see an external problem and be swayed by my thoughts and reactions. I have to intentionally fix my eyes on Jesus amidst the storms of life. Jesus is cheering me on, longing for me to focus my eyes on His. He knows it will go well for me when I leap into His outstretched arms.

Father told me recently:

> *"I am with you every step of the way.*

I am beside you and behind you.

I walk in front of you paving the way.

I am leading you.

Take my hand and follow Me.

C'mon, baby girl, you can do this!"

"Why, my soul, are you downcast? Why so disturbed within me? Put your hope in God, for I will yet praise him, my Savior and my God." Psalm 43:5 NIV

Section Two
God's Love

Chapter Six:

The With-ness of God

Waiting in line for a night of worship in San Diego, California, talking with the couple in front of me increased my anticipation. I believed the six-hour drive, reserving a hotel room and taking the time to show up would be worth it. When the venue doors opened, conversations paused, and everybody faced toward the entrance with expectation. Following the crowd through the lobby and the second set of double doors, the introvert in me scanned the room and gasped. There were no seats, just an empty room with instruments on an elevated stage.

I'm the type of person who chooses an aisle seat in a theater, auditorium or airplane. I like having space next to me. With this sold-out worship night, I pictured us looking like a can of sardines. The idea of getting packed into a room with wall-to-wall people made me tense. Fortunately, I found a small square area with an iron railing halfway back from the stage. Positioning myself in the front corner of this empty platform helped me feel more relaxed.

Once worship began, I closed my eyes to block out the distraction of all the people. My ears welcomed the pleasant sound of worship. With hands and voices raised collectively, the presence of God filled the room.

During worship, Holy Spirit gave me a picture of being underwater:

Deep in an ocean at night, with no land in sight, I wasn't alone. Either Jesus or an angelic being swam in tandem above me as if swimming freestyle. This swimmer, who appeared as a silhouette from a bystander's view, propelled me gently through the water.

At one point, I looked up toward the moonlit surface, calculating its distance and wondering when I'd need to breathe. Somehow, I knew that wouldn't be necessary if I trusted this swimming companion. It was as if I had the choice whether to surface at will or go deeper in trust. If I chose to go deeper, I sensed new sights and treasures awaited.

Still, my analytical mind wondered if I could proceed to the ocean depths without taking in any oxygen. Within seconds a decision had to be made, go up toward known safety or down to the unknown.

I chose to go deeper. We effortlessly moved through the water, gliding and descending. That inner tug to get to the surface no longer pulled at me. An unexpected brightness came into view as we headed downward, sparking my curiosity. Our descent took us to the bottom of the ocean that teemed with marine life and what looked like shiny jewelry. Fish of all kinds, colors of a wide variety and light of a unique hue encompassed what should have been a deep dark abyss.

After that spectacular scene, my eyes opened, bringing me back to the worship night in San Diego. Whoa, I felt different. Something internally had changed with my decision to go deeper. Experiencing that underwater scene increased my expectation of a hope-filled future I couldn't yet see. Isn't that what faith is? "Now faith is confidence in what we hope for and assurance about what we do not see." Hebrews 11:1 NIV

One of the future things I had not foreseen, but experienced since then, was leading worship at a friend's outdoor house church. Bright yellow and orange leaves wafted from the trees surrounding the spacious backyard patio where everyone gathered. The brisk morning air made me mindful of keeping my hands in my jacket pockets; I didn't want my fingers to be numb when it came time to play my guitar.

After everyone settled in their seats and my friend introduced me, I segued into worship. "Today, I'm moved by the fact that God is with us. He is with us. Not only that but also, Psalm 23:6 says, 'Surely goodness and mercy will follow me all the days of my life.' Goodness and mercy will follow us ALL the days of our lives. His goodness is incredible!" My voice cracked and tears welled up.

Deep breath. Exhale.

Regaining my composure by playing several bars of the opening worship song, I sang out, and we declared His goodness. By the end of the worship time, faith had increased, powerful prayers had been prayed and healing was released. Our compassionate God met with us in tangible ways that morning.

The next morning as I rolled out of bed, I still felt the "with-ness" of God. My heart felt tender and filled to overflowing. My pen could barely write fast enough as these words of praise and thanksgiving spilled onto my journal page:

"I am so arrested by Your goodness!

You are my very breath, my heart, my soul, in whom I place my trust.

You are forever!

You are just. You are merciful and the One in whom my soul delights!

You are careful to lead me in the way everlasting.

You take into consideration my tenderness and vulnerability.

Thank you, God! I praise You with all of my being. I give You my heart, soul, mind and strength!

I bless You, Father, with everything that is within me. You bless me by Your very presence. Thank you for Your "with-ness" wherever I go.

I praise and thank you for making me unique and a carrier of Your presence. Your life-giving Spirit compels me forward.

I love You. I serve You. I honor You. I give myself completely to You!"

Similarly, God's "with-ness" also lingered when I went to Thailand several years ago. At a resort in the Chiang Mai Province, our team hosted a three-day women's conference. The second day's teaching session neared its end as the missionary women listened intently. Standing in back of the dimly lit ballroom, I prayed silently, and a picture of Jesus putting His hands through my extended hands came to mind. He assured me that when I laid hands on people in prayer, His healing hands touched them.

Knowing Jesus wanted to heal people through my hands increased my confidence to pray in faith, believing. I felt a boost of courage from this experience with Him. At this conference, each person Holy Spirit led me to felt His healing touch. Thank you, Lord!

"Have I not commanded you? Be strong and courageous! Do not be terrified nor dismayed, for the Lord your God is with you wherever you go." Joshua 1:9

Recently, I got this additional revelation of God's "with-ness" as I sat in my recliner spending the morning with Him.

Picture the Matterhorn ride at Disneyland, where one person sits in front of the other in a bobsled. Father positioned Himself behind me as if we sat in a bobsled. Seated in front of Him, hands clutching my opened Bible, I read First Corinthians 12:7 TPT, "Each believer is given continuous revelation by the Holy Spirit to benefit not just himself but all."

I sensed His delight and felt His arms extended, underneath mine. Being with Him and reading Scripture felt good. My heart responded with overflowing affection for Him. Again, His presence got me misty-eyed, and I lingered.

A little while later, I glanced at the clock, and saw it was time to get to work. Gratitude overwhelmed me, and I said aloud, "Thank you, God, for being with me!" My body felt tingly when I changed seats to the computer desk in the living room. Immanuel, one of God's names, means *God with us*. His "with-ness" remained as I went into my online meetings and throughout the afternoon.

"Therefore the Lord Himself will give you a sign: Behold, the virgin will conceive and give birth to a son, and she will name Him Immanuel." Isaiah 7:14

Chapter Seven:

Everlasting Love

"The Lord appeared to him long ago, saying, "I have loved you with an everlasting love; Therefore, I have drawn you with lovingkindness." Jeremiah 31:3

How many times have I read this verse, and yet the richness and depth of its meaning didn't hit me? Have you ever read a familiar passage in the Bible, and one day, it's as if your eyes are seeing it for the first time? You get it! The author's intent suddenly becomes clear, and you receive it.

Sometimes in the morning, toward the end of my time with the Lord, I write, "What Else Lord?" on my journal page. Then I remain quiet and listen. He reminds me of how much He loves me or tells me how He sees me, solidifying my identity in Him.

Reading my "What Else Lord" sections in past journal entries, I discovered that in the span of six months, God told me 33 times, "I love you with an everlasting love." It wasn't until the 33rd time when I got the revelation of "everlasting." I wrote in my journal, "Not only is Your love everlasting, but it's also previous! All of my earthly relationships have a starting point. (My husband and I met in Hawaii in 1989. My kids each have a birthdate.) You knew me before I was born!"

"Your eyes have seen my formless substance; And in Your book were written, all the days that were ordained *for me,* when as yet there was not one of them." Psalm 139:16

Here are words from Father, captured in my journal pages:

"You are My precious daughter in whom My soul delights. The affection I have for you surpasses that of all the ones who love you on earth. I am your Prince of Peace, Everlasting Father (Isaiah 9:6), *King of Kings and Lord of lords.*

I AM the One who loves you most! I indeed love you with an everlasting love! My love has no starting point nor ending point. I've always loved you!"

I cried when it hit me that God had always loved me, even before I was born (Psalm 139:16). I missed this revelation previously because I read the declaration as:

"I LOVE you with an everlasting love."

"I love YOU with an everlasting love."

"I LOVE YOU with an everlasting love."

Finally, I got it:

"I love YOU with an EVERLASTING LOVE!"

"Father's love for me has no starting point, and better yet, no ending point! This is huge! No one else loves as He loves.

I am undone!

I feel seen!

I feel known!

54

I feel loved!

I am His Beloved!

Thank you, Lord, for deepening my understanding of Your love!"

Fast forward seven months to an online meeting with my life coach. I was in *efficiency mode* because of wanting to discuss several topics in the allotted 50-minute time slot. When in this frame of mind, my emotions get tucked away. Because I'm hardwired to function analytically, excelling at handling details, creating systems for reaching goals and coming up with solutions, this is my default way of being efficient.

Even though my coach asked helpful questions to take me deeper into the topics I initiated, I responded from my head, not my heart. The issues we discussed were heart-focused, but I didn't allow my emotions to go there. That is, until I read aloud to my coach what God told me in a recent journal entry:

"I love you with an everlasting love.

I have clothed you with lovingkindness.

It is My delight to be your wraparound presence.

You are not unprotected."

My voice cracked, and my composure softened.

"I love you with an everlasting love."

Deep breath. Exhale slowly. I felt my body relax as I pictured myself seated on Father's lap, held in His loving embrace. His wraparound presence coaxed my lurking heart to come out of the shadows.

"God's glory is all around me! His wraparound presence is all I need, for the Lord is my Savior, my hero, and my life-giving strength." Psalm 62:7 TPT

In the warmth of His presence, I felt safe, secure, and filled with His love. While on that Zoom call, my heart showed up for the conversation, and my coach was better able to steer me in the right direction.

Later in the day, I journaled what had taken place in the coaching call. I wonder how my days would look if I consistently remembered He loves me like it says in Ephesians?

"And continue to walk surrendered to the extravagant love of Christ, for he surrendered his life as a sacrifice for us. His great love for us was pleasing to God, like an aroma of adoration-a sweet healing fragrance." Ephesians 5:2 TPT

> "Walking surrendered." Ponder that one. Walking yielded. How in the world is that possible? It can sound exposing and feel vulnerable. For me, I need to feel safe to live surrendered. I feel safe when I feel valued and loved.
>
> Psalm 139:17-18 TPT reminds me of God's heart toward me.
>
> "Every single moment, you are thinking of me!
>
> How precious and wonderful to consider
>
> that you cherish me constantly in your every thought!
>
> O God, your desires toward me are more

than the grains of sand on every shore!

When I awake each morning, you're still with me."

"Ahh, to keep this truth at the forefront of my mind. I just got a picture of Father standing near me, gazing at me with a smile. I feel His acceptance. I sense His delight. I bask in His love. He does, indeed, love me with an everlasting love. I can walk surrendered."

Chapter Eight:

Transformation

Calling from nearly 5,400 miles away in Japan, my young adult daughter, who is an experienced traveler, said, "My flight got canceled, and there are no more flights out tonight. My phone is at 13%!" She was over an hour away from the airport and didn't know where to stay overnight.

Typically, she'd handle travel changes on her own, so her reaching out alerted me that the situation was unusual, and I heard the urgency in her voice. Feeling uncertain and pressured to speak concisely because of her low cell phone battery, I knew I had two choices.

Usually, I'd go into problem-solving mode: asking clarifying questions to formulate a plan. After all, event planning which entails a lot of problem-solving, is part of my life experience. However, I'm in the process of learning a second option. It requires surrendering my analytical mind, pausing and asking God what to do. Crying out to Him needs to be my first step, not my second option.

After a quick, silent prayer, while keeping my ear glued to my cell phone, I asked my daughter, "What can I do to help?" Inwardly I thought, "Whoa, Holy Spirit, that was unexpected and good!" My daughter told me what she needed, and I responded that I'd text her the answers. Then we hung up. I quickly found the information she wanted and texted her. She called the airline and got booked on a different flight out that same night. Problem solved.

Weeks after this incident, we talked about the phone call from Japan. My daughter commented that she was thankful for my response. It's those moments in parenting when I breathe a sigh of relief and feel deep gratitude. Finding an alternative to her canceled flight was my daughter's problem to solve, yet I was able to contribute a piece of information she requested.

Thank you, Holy Spirit, for prompting me to ask that one question rather than rattle off irrelevant questions in an attempt to gain information and suggest possible solutions.

"For My thoughts are not your thoughts, nor are your ways, My ways,' declares the Lord. 'For as the heavens are higher than the earth, so are My ways higher than your ways and My thoughts than your thoughts." Isaiah 55:8-9

Another scenario that required an atypical response from me took place on an errand I ran for my husband. He needed some additional stain for our backyard fence because the dry boards drank his previously purchased gallons faster than anticipated. Two more gallons were needed.

I headed to our local paint store and took my place in line near the aisles of paint cans and accessories. I was the first person in line, but the client in front of me took a long time getting the items he needed. With only one clerk working the counter, I had no choice but to wait. Honestly, I had the fleeting thought of leaving and returning another time, but I sensed the Lord wanted me to remain.

What happened next was not something I'd ever done before. When the cashier was standing at the cash register, I looked at her and prayed silently, "God, how do you want to love on her today?" For some reason I repeated the question under my breath, "God, how do you want to love on her today?" I'm a question asker by nature, but I'd never stood in a line and asked that question before. An inner transformation was taking place without me realizing it. Within seconds, He gave me a download of what to communicate to the cashier when it became my turn at the counter.

Fairly soon afterward, the customer left. I walked up to the counter and ordered the two gallons of stain my husband needed. Inwardly I was praying for the right timing of when to mention the promise God had for her. I noticed another customer had entered the store and was waiting in line. We finished the transaction, and I slid my credit card back into my pocket. Right then, I knew it was time.

Not wanting the other customer to hear, I leaned toward the cashier, looked her in the eyes, and said in a hushed voice, "The Lord sees what you're going through and what concerns you." The clerk exclaimed with a nervous chuckle, "Am I wearing it on my face?" I answered that sometimes the Lord tells me things to encourage people. I told her the rest of the message and a Bible verse to go along with it.

She came around the counter with my two gallons of stain and walked beside me toward the store's front door. As we walked, a question came out of my mouth that I hadn't anticipated, nor had I previously asked in this context. With a tender heart, evidence of Father's love, I asked her, "Do you know Him?"

She responded with a sparkle in her eyes, "Yes, I know Him!" Her countenance changed to one of joy and gratitude.

Once outside my van, she told me how she knew Him and what He had done for her. Then, she kindly set the stain on my floorboard. I asked if I could pray a blessing over her, to which she said a hearty, "Yes." After the "Amen," she bounded back into the store with a huge grin on her face. Her countenance changed because of an unexpected promise God delivered to her at her workplace. God is so good!

One other area where God is changing my default in is my awareness of my emotional state. The other morning, something felt "off." I could tell I wasn't engaging with Father meaningfully. As I was about to question Him about it, I got a picture of a thin transparent barrier over my heart. It was like a sheet of plastic covering my heart to protect it. But why did I feel the need for self-protection? I didn't know.

I did my usual reading in Proverbs, but no verses leapt off the page at me. I read some pages from a book on intercessory prayer. They were a good read, but nothing worth noting in my journal. My heart remained veiled.

Finally, I wrote in my journal:

"Lord, I have to be honest. I'm feeling a little protective skin over my heart, and I don't know why."

After writing several paragraphs, I asked Him if I needed to do something to remove this protective film. He answered:

"Cast your cares on Me for I care for you (1 Peter 5:7). *Write down all your cares."*

Underneath the heading, "My cares," I wrote five things that were on my mind. The first one had to do with Thanksgiving – wanting it to be fun and meaningful for our family. The last one had to do with my upcoming birthday and wondering how it would be without the friends who had moved out of state.

"I will especially miss the one whom I've had a birthday lunch with for the past 15 years."

"Will you trust Me to make it special for you?"

"Yes, of course!"

"Will you place each of these cares into my hands?"

I pictured Him standing in front of Me, hands outstretched, palms up, inviting me to transfer my cares to Him. I sensed Father had a plan for each one and willingly placed all five into His outstretched hands.

Thank you, Lord, that You are changing my ways, my internal default settings. Transformation is happening while You direct my paths (Proverbs 3:5-6). I trust You!

Chapter Nine:

Invitation to Comfort

Waking up and getting to my usual spot with the Lord felt like any other morning. I eagerly grabbed my Bible and read a chapter in Proverbs. Wanting to give room for Holy Spirit to uncover a deeper meaning, I closed my eyes to think about the passage and waited. What happened next surprised me!

In my mind, I got a picture of Father God stroking my hair as I sat on His lap. I felt awkward because I was not used to being comforted by physical affection. Receiving love in this way is near the bottom of my love language list, and my stiffness revealed my discomfort. As if coaching myself through it, I thought, "My first step is to relax. Then, take some deep breaths."

After taking a few breaths, I carefully leaned my head on His shoulder. Immediately, the tension in my body released. Yesterday's sadness and disappointment lightened as I nestled in close to Him. It reminded me of an inflated balloon releasing its air pressure. Cared for and comforted, I relaxed in Father's presence.

I didn't know how much time passed, but I decided to capture this experience in my journal. Because I often have two-way conversations with God in writing, I felt compelled to ask, "What are You inviting me into today?" Within seconds, the word "comfort" came to mind. My heart warmed, and I thought, "Oh, how sweet! That's the lovingkindness of my

Father!" Putting my journal aside, I leaned in closer and lingered.

A few minutes later, thoughts about one of my close friends, Leslie, moving out of state evoked my sadness from the day before. Although I had known her plans to move for several weeks, I hadn't felt the emotional impact until a mutual friend asked for photos for a personalized gift book. With each image discovered on my phone, I remembered how good it felt to be with my friend having fun and exploring nature.

Leslie and I prayed and took communion beside a river on two separate adventures. Another time, we picnicked amidst the sequoia trees and snow-covered ground. That same day, I noticed a lone butterfly flying around me as we headed back to the car. I set my phone to camera mode and tried to get a picture, but the butterfly flitted about too swiftly. Finally, I decided to stand still with my camera posed in my hands, thinking I'd take a picture when it flew past my lens.

Within seconds, the wild butterfly didn't just fly past, but like a piece of metal sticking to a magnet, it landed on my finger! I quickly got Leslie's attention to take a picture with her camera. She carefully moved in close and captured the unforgettable moment!

Although grateful for the memories made in the mountains, parks and gardens, my emotions sank deeper into a feeling of loss. Sadness set in, as I contemplated moments like these with my friend coming to an end. That same day, I received a text from her saying she and her husband had put an offer on a new house. Right then, the reality of her move hit me like a ton of bricks.

When Leslie initially told me she was moving, she'd had a few days to process the change. Although she knew the timing was right for the move, she felt sad about leaving her friends. I responded encouragingly, "We'll keep in touch!" I didn't feel sad yet because I hadn't had time to process the news.

It took my personal coach saying the word "grief" to help me realize I was grieving. I told her how my friend was good at getting me to go outside in nature. She helped me take breaks from my work, and I welcomed her invitations to play.

Knowing I am an internal processor, my coach gave me some homework. She suggested asking myself this question: Why does it bother me so much that my friend is leaving? She told me that as I followed the thread of asking what I'll miss about my friend, I'd end up with a reason that's about me.

Not having done this exercise before, I was intrigued and willing to work through it. After the coaching call ended, I grabbed a pen and my journal and got comfortable in the nearest chair. Here is how my journal entry began:

"We are spontaneous with each other.

Nine times out of ten, when one of us asks if we want to do something, the other is available.

It's a very comfortable friendship in that we share the deepest and the silliest parts of ourselves with each other."

There were a few more components to this thread, but as my coach predicted, this exercise revealed the underlying reason for my profoundly emotional response. Captured in my journal was this unveiling moment:

"With her going away, I don't have anyone in town who

is caught up with my life. That's not true. It's not like I'll be left unknown by everyone. Is that my fear, no one will know me once she moves? Do I fear not being known by anybody? Yep, that's it. She's on the inside circle. To lose her is difficult for me."

I marveled how this simple exercise had worked to uncover a deep-seated need in me that I had never verbalized. I discovered my need to feel known. Whoa, that's vulnerable and raw, and honestly, a bit scary.

Now, I understood why Father gave me an invitation to comfort that very morning. He knew what my day held, and He knew I would need His comforting presence. I am known to Him. He is my very present help in trouble (Psalm 46:1b). This alerted me to begin asking God each morning, "God, what are You inviting me into today?"

The next day, in a phone conversation with a different friend, I told her I had recently discovered a question I wanted to add to my daily practices. I didn't tell her the picture of God comforting me; I only told her the question, "God, what are You inviting me into today?"

At the end of our call, we prayed for each other. She alluded to the question and prayed that I'd partner with God as I went about my day. I thought, "Yes, she got it!" Asking this question postured my heart to partner with God as I went about my day.

"All praises belong to the God and Father of our Lord Jesus Christ. For He is the Father of tender mercy and the God of endless comfort. He always comes alongside us to comfort us in every suffering so that we can come alongside those who are in any painful trial. We can bring them this same comfort that

God has poured out upon us. And just as we experience the abundance of Christ's own sufferings, even more of God's comfort will cascade upon us through our union with Christ."
2 Corinthians 1:3-4 TPT

Chapter Ten:

Handpicked by God

In 2020, while praying in my living room, a friend imagined a picture of God opening a drawer of a tall file cabinet, reaching in and pulling out a file with my name on it. This picture came as my friend sat on the couch opposite me and prayed for my writing process. Her prayers were encouragement from God that He would lead me as I attempted to write my first book, the book you're now reading.

In the coming days following that prayer moment, I sat with hands poised over the computer keyboard, eyes closed, ready to document whatever God told me from those files. Story after story from my childhood got recounted as I took dictation.

One of the early childhood stories took place in the mountains. My older brother gave me a ride on his new Mini Enduro motorcycle. I don't know if this incident contributed to the fact that I have my motorcycle license today. But I wonder. After completing this file, I checked with my brother about the details to see if what I was hearing was correct. He confirmed his age, the motorcycle and the location of my childhood memory. What I was sensing from the Lord was accurate, and these events, most of which I didn't remember, actually happened.

Here's the kicker: I had completely forgotten about these files on my computer until late one night in 2021 when I came across an old journal entry while searching for something else. As I read a short line in the journal about Jesus revealing a file to me, I vaguely recalled saving files on my computer like that.

The next day, with great anticipation, I sat at my computer desk and clicked on "Find" to locate the forgotten files. I tried typing different words into the search bar, but nothing led me to the forgotten treasure. Frustrated, I had no idea where I stored those files. After exhausting a search of my 2020 electronic folder, I started poking around a different folder.

Finally, I found them in the "Book Listening" folder. Note to self: rename the folder, so it's easier to find!

Still not remembering the folder's contents, I clicked on the "Book Listening" icon with expectation. Suddenly, 37 document icons popped up in that "Book Listening" folder. Yes, 37! What a wealth of possible stories for my book! Locating the specific file mentioned in my old journal, I clicked on it with bated breath.

Whoa, it all started coming back. When I had trouble writing, I met with God and asked Him which file He wanted to show me. As I closed my eyes, I saw Him smile as He opened a manila file folder, which raised my sense of anticipation. I never knew what to expect, but I believed it would be for my good.

Sometimes I saw bright beams of light coming out of a file. I'm not sure what those meant, but He was unflinching, so I figured it was fine. Most times, He leaned one elbow on the edge of the tall file cabinet as a particular file lay open in His hands. As He viewed the file contents, the look on His face reflected the love He had in His heart for me.

Although unconventional, I want to share with you the interaction between Father and me as He revealed the contents of one of those precious files. I sat near Him as He invited me to learn the truth about my birth story. Here is our conversation about "File 4 Oct 16."

As I pictured Father standing in front of the tall file cabinet, looking into the open file folder in His hands, I asked Him:

"What are you reading?"

"I'm reading how you were a much-loved child. You were wanted and waited for by your father and mother. I put a longing in their hearts for a third child, and you were it, My daughter."

Hmm, wow! Thank you, Father!

"You've heard your mom tell the story of how they were going to adopt, but then she got pregnant with you. They wanted you! You had and still have a place in your family of origin put there by Me! I chose your family placement and your specific family. Do you recognize My handiwork in that choice?"

Well, I wondered if I had been an afterthought, an accident even. There was such an age difference between my brother and me. But when I asked my mom about it, she said they would've adopted had she not gotten pregnant.

"You were not an afterthought. You were in My heart long before you showed up on earth. I love you with everlasting love, My child."

So, the reality is, You formed my identity long before I came to earth.

"Your grandmother was delighted to have another granddaughter. I saw her smiling at the news of your birth. She was at the hospital when you were born."

"Really?"

"Yes! You are a part of a legacy of strong women.

Your grandmother was tough and tender at the same time. Do you remember how kind she was to you?"

"Yes, I do. Grandma was sweet to me and soft-spoken from what I can remember."

"Yes, but she had an inner strength that is also in you. The kind that is resilient, firm, steadfast and consistent.'

"I had no idea."

"Thank you for my heritage, God. I'm taking it all in as You unveil the story of my life. I feel like You are reframing the narrative that I've ignored about my early life and my family of origin.

You are my Living Hope, God!

Thank you, God, that You picked the family I'd be born into before I came to this earth.

You looked and saw that they were incomplete without me.

I am not an afterthought, a mistake or an unwanted child.

I am Your child, hand-picked by My Creator.

Thank you, Father, for my identity; first in Your family,

Then in the family on earth that You picked for me.

You are worthy, worthy, worthy God.

I worship You and bow down before You.

I acknowledge You as Lord and King over my life.

I surrender, I give You all of me,

the known and unknown parts of me.

You created and formed me in my mother's womb at the right time.

You picked my birthdate.

You knew I'd always be the youngest one in every class because I skipped Kindergarten.

That was Your providence.

I love You, Lord. I acknowledge that You know best!

You want the best for me!

You have my best interests at heart every time.

I can trust You!

You are Lord of my life, and I willingly give you everything.

Thank you for reframing where necessary.

I trust You to continue that work in due time.

You are the God of the breakthrough!"

"Thank you for your heart, Little One.

You are My one and only Sandi Sadako.

I treasure you.

You are in the palm of My hand (Isaiah 49:16).

I have clothed you in lovingkindness (Colossians 3:12 NIV).

I rescued you from the mire (Psalm 40:2 NIV).

Where unseen forces were seeking to destroy you

and avert your destiny, I have won you!

I have kept you from being buried alive

before you had a chance to shine, to thrive.

You are walking in this thriving period.

It's the start of more to come,

more than you can imagine.

You don't have to strive or stress; you have to let yourself get carried away by Me.

I have plans and purposes that are getting revealed now.

You are on the verge of something huge!"

"Oh God, thank you for your promises!

You have my whole heart! I'm here, fully showing up.

I am not holding back any part of me.

You hold me in Your arms; I am in life union with You.

Thank you, God! I love You!"

Section Three
God's Heart

Chapter Eleven:

The Look

In the quietness of the morning, what I saw took me by surprise and filled me with love. Tottering between sleeping and being fully awake, I got a glimpse of Father God smiling at me with a twinkle in His eyes. I had never seen that look before. It was different than His familiar look of delight. Before I opened my eyes, my heart suddenly flooded with clarity and warmth. Through the expression on His face, Father communicated He was proud of me!

I was astounded, because this *I'm proud of you* look wasn't attached to any action on my part. Typically, someone is proud of another because of a good performance, demonstration of character or some other behavior. But this, this was a pure declaration from my Father who wanted to bless His beloved daughter at the beginning of her day.

My body felt a surge of warmth as if receiving a hug from God Himself. I felt loved and seen like never before. This unexpected affirmation gave me an extra burst of energy. The affection I felt lingered with me the rest of the day, and everything seemed easier.

Knowing God was proud of me helped tame my nerves as I played the keyboard with a worship leader I'd not led with before. The worship leader's keyboardist had canceled half a day before the event. I like to feel prepared, so stepping into the situation last-minute was potentially nerve-wracking. Remembering Father's *I'm proud of you* look earlier that morning made all the difference.

Now, whenever I say yes to new opportunities, especially the big ones, I'm reminded that it's not about me and my need to feel prepared. My performance is never in question. There is nothing I can do to make God love me more and nothing I can do to make Him love me less. My Father is proud of me.

When writing in my journal the other day, I wrote down my feelings about the ebb and flow of some friendships in my life. Although relationship changes are inevitable, they never seem to come at convenient or expected times. As my analytical mind tried to make sense of these transitions, Father broke into my thoughts and once again said, "I'm proud of you!" Oh, how I needed that!

Father's words changed my whole countenance. I felt His nearness. He reminded me I was not alone, and He saw what I was going through. I felt understood and comforted as I rested in the arms of my Father. The discomfort of the friendship transitions didn't go away, but the sting of the changes became less painful.

Several weeks later, I was wading through work projects on my home computer and found myself distracted. My emotions were rising to the surface, begging for some form of expression. Usually, I'd grab my journal and write, but I felt led to do something different. I opened a new document and typed, "Lord, what do You want to say to me now?"

Here is what He said:

"I want to tell you that I'm proud of you. You are persevering through a difficult situation, and you are letting Me lead you through your emotional heart growth. I know it is not easy for you to feel and give place to your emotions, but I created you to feel, not just think. You are a complete, whole being, Beloved. You need your heart as well as your head."

Later, He said this:

"I've got perfect timing. Don't despair or despise the process. It is necessary for growth, like toothpaste being squeezed out of the toothpaste tube. Pressure is applied to get the good stuff out for its intended assignment.

Let Me train and teach you.

Remain open to Me and to the process, even when it's painful.

Just as fast-growing bones can cause growing pains in a child's body, accelerated growth in you is uncomfortable.

It doesn't mean anything is wrong.

It just means you are gaining the necessary internal skills you'll need for future assignments.

Rest and revel in Me.

Sitting with Me in the Secret Place is the best thing you can do in this season.

In fact, this is where you need to remain in any season.

I am your hope and stay.

I am your bright shining future.

I know how to get you to where you are going.

Trust Me in how we get there."

My heart exploded; God was proud of me even in difficult learning situations. I'm so thankful for this truth. He's teaching me that I don't have to figure out these challenging situations before sitting with Him. In the midst of not understanding what's going on, I can linger with Him. He is proud of me and wants to be with me.

In recent years, I've noticed my husband intentionally communicating his heart to each of our young-adult children. Most recently, our son stopped in for a visit and sat on the couch in our living room. My husband, sitting on the keyboard bench, facing our son, made a point of saying how proud he was of him. As a parent observing this interaction, I felt gratitude. My husband understands the value of speaking words of life to our children, who are now adults.

Even more so, my Heavenly Father intentionally reminds me that He is proud of me. Sometimes He whispers it in my ear. Other times, I remember the look I saw on His face in the quietness of the morning. Anytime He does it, my heart soars, and whatever troubles I'm facing shrink in complexity. It's as if He interrupts my thoughts to remind me He loves me and is with me.

Psalm 17:8 says, "Keep me as the apple of the eye; hide me in the shadow of Your wings."

In the Cambridge Dictionary, that colloquialism, "apple of the eye," means the person who someone loves most and is very proud of. I believe David, the writer of Psalm 17, was familiar with Father's *I'm proud of you* look.

When this look comes to mind, I remember how God sees me in every circumstance. I am the apple of His eye! Declare this over yourself. I am the apple of His eye!

Chapter Twelve:

Fearfully and Wonderfully Made

While sitting in my usual morning spot with Bible and journal open on my lap, God started an unexpected conversation with me. I heard Him say:

> *It's time to let the hidden part of your identity out, to look at it; be aware of it; learn from it; accept it.*
>
> *Do you believe you are fearfully and wonderfully made?"* (Psalm 139:14)

Stunned, I stammered an unsteady, "Yes," without owning it. I suddenly felt fidgety in my comfortable blue recliner. What was happening? What did He mean by "hidden part"?

Next, God led me to recall and process through an elementary school incident that still carried an edge of ignored emotional residue:

I saw the metal merry-go-round, horizontal bars and swings atop the hard dirt playground. Kids were playing in scattered groups. Painted hopscotch lines on the asphalt had girls hopping from square to square. It felt good to be outside during recess.

The scene froze on two main characters, a brown-haired boy with big, round eyes and me with short black hair at age seven or eight. I don't know which direction he came from, but the brown-haired boy stood abruptly in front of me on the dirt playground. I didn't see any other kids near him, so he didn't seem to be playing a game.

It all happened so fast. The boy looked me squarely in the face and chanted, "Chinese, Japanese, dirty knees," and I can't say the rest. My brain scrambled to grasp what was happening. Nobody had ever made comments about my Asian eyes. I felt something unfamiliar. All of a sudden, I felt different; I didn't look like the other kids.

There weren't any teachers nearby who had witnessed this life-altering scene. No one defended me. The boy ran off, and I took an invisible yet scathing arrow to my heart. Minutes after the incident, my mind came up with verbal responses that didn't make it out of my mouth. I hadn't yet learned the art of sarcasm or comebacks. Instead, I internalized the searing pain of the verbal assault. The way I looked at the world changed that day. I no longer existed in a safe, kind world.

The bell rang, signifying the end of recess. My heart was heavy, and my head spun as I sauntered toward the line of students waiting on the asphalt. Entering the classroom, I didn't see the boy anywhere. My mind reeled from being singled out for something I couldn't change and didn't choose. Feelings of rejection and shame flooded my heart because of my Japanese-American eyes.

Sitting at my desk, I wondered why hadn't I said anything to the boy? I came up with a few good lines, but none escaped my lips. Nor did I tell my teacher. I was alone in this battle. I was on my own to make myself feel okay.

When I got home that afternoon, my mom asked about my school day. I shrugged it off as just another day. Feeling the sting of my wounded heart, I couldn't bring myself to repeat what had happened. That day, I learned my differences made me vulnerable, and my heart could bruise. From that point on, I kept my heart safe by keeping it hidden, protected.

Changing elementary schools a few years later allowed me to show up as my wiser, protected self. My fifth-grade self figured out that the way to gain respect from peers was to do things well.

The black asphalt play area at my new school lent itself to activities such as four-square, dodgeball, tetherball and double-Dutch jump rope. My friend and I were the best at double-Dutch, counting the number of consecutive jumps into the hundreds. No one said anything unkind to me at this school.

Excelling in academics, especially math and English, fed my competitive drive. I held the record for the fastest time in completing 100 multiplication equations correctly. I felt accepted by classmates and supported by teachers. I kept in contact with my fifth-grade math teacher and sixth-grade homeroom teacher long after my years at this elementary school. They took interest in my life and appreciated when I stopped by to say, "Hello."

This achievement mindset served me well throughout the rest of my public-school years. It was the best way I knew to feel accepted and respected. Newspaper articles, sports awards and academic recognition reinforced my strategy. My performance orientation drove my need to improve my game. If I threw a wild pitch in softball or missed an easy shot in basketball, I scolded myself. I became my worst critic and my best motivator.

Sitting in my familiar recliner, having this childhood recollection, I knew what God was asking of me. He wanted me to shed my self-made protective armor, the one I created to cover my wounded heart. He had shown me time and time again how He saw me. Nearly every day for the past year, He told me how deeply He loves me. He often reminded me that I don't need my self-protection; I've got Him as my protector.

He's always been my rock, fortress and deliverer (Psalm 18:2). It was time to choose Him as the protector of my vulnerable heart.

I had learned to keep my heart safe by letting my analytical mind take the lead. Now, it was time to live with emotions and thoughts integrated. It was decades after the inflicted heart wound, and I felt ready to let go of my self-protective persona.

Two weeks later, when I visited a church in Los Angeles, the pastor preached from Psalm 23. Sitting outside, green grass under feet, tarp overhead to keep me shaded, my heart resonated with the pastor's words. I noted his words, "Many times we don't feel protected because we're protecting ourselves." He summarized the point: "Let God protect and vindicate you." It was no accident I visited that Sunday. The Good Shepherd wanted to do a deeper heart healing.

During his closing prayer, this father-hearted pastor encouraged everyone to allow God to identify areas needing His healing touch. I took a deep breath, closed my eyes and felt an expectancy as I waited to hear from God. Within seconds, I revisited the playground scene from my childhood. I saw the boy from my elementary school standing several feet in front of me. Jesus entered the scene and stood between the boy and me, facing the boy. I didn't know what He said, but I knew Jesus loved the boy.

Next, Jesus turned toward me and removed the arrow sticking out of my heart, the one that landed there when the boy hurled unkind words at me. Jesus gently put His hand on my heart and healed the wound left by the dislodged arrow. I believed He sealed the wound rather than making it disappear. I understood this because I have other scars that Father once told me are beauty marks. My heart got a beauty mark that day.

After talking and praying with a sweet young couple who sat behind me during service, I walked toward the courtyard to say goodbye to a friend. After getting over the surprise of seeing me, we chatted for a few minutes, and I told her what happened during the closing prayer. She prayed for me, and I received encouragement to keep leaning into all God had for me.

Several weeks later, considering the emotional healing taking place, a picture of a newly emergent butterfly came to mind. It had purple wings that were damp from wriggling out of the chrysalis. At first, this young butterfly flew erratically because the wings had not dried. I also felt unsteady and unsure while attempting to take flight.

Here is what God spoke to my heart about this growth season:

> *"I made you to feel deeply.*
> *I've created you to have joy, peace and My presence.*
> *I made you to feel deeply, to enjoy My company and the company of others.*
> *You've buried your deeper innermost self for so long.*
> *Now, it's time to let her out. She's lovely, really.*
> *You can get to know her now.*
>
> *It's safe for you to come out and let yourself be seen.*

You don't have to remain hidden.
You can trust who I've surrounded you with.
They will support you as you explore the freedom of
expression."
My response:
"Nothing is holding me back!
No more hiding!
No more keeping a lid on it!
No more lessening my responses!
No more squelching my heart expressions out of fear of
being awkward or conspicuous!

Thank you! I feel as if the starting gate has flung wide
open, and it's time to take off running!"

With deepening resolve, I say, "I am fearfully and
wonderfully made."

Chapter Thirteen:

All That Delights His Heart

"Beloved friends, what should be our proper response to God's marvelous mercies? To surrender yourselves to God to be his sacred, living sacrifices. And live in holiness, experiencing all that delights his heart. For this becomes your genuine expression of worship." Romans 12:1 TPT

One morning, curiosity led me to ask Father, "What delights Your heart?" I had read Romans 12:1 earlier, and the phrase "experiencing all that delights his heart" caught my eye.

As I closed my eyes, I pictured Father inviting me to walk with Him. I didn't know where, but I sensed the value was in spending time with Him, enjoying His company. I didn't need to know, for I was content to be with Him and Jesus. We left our spot on the grassy knoll and walked on a path that looked like dark green, emerald moss, or maybe green gummy bear paste. It was glossy, yet not sticky. As we walked, I tried to describe the experience but lacked the words.

After walking with Him for a bit, I saw a white city with pointed, gothic architecture in the distance and paused. Within seconds we stood on the edge of a city filled with tall, white, iridescent buildings, even though we hadn't taken steps to get there. Father wanted to show me a specific place and instructed me to wear my earbuds.

We walked through the narrow hallways bathed in a calming, blueish-lavender light. I couldn't hear a sound as my hands brushed the walls made of a thin white, seashell-like material. Large round holes in the walls like portal windows gave me glimpses into other spaces. Although the passageways were relatively narrow, I easily followed my hosts.

Father led me into a large open room, like a concert hall. The first instrument I noticed was stage left and appeared to be a cello cradled in a stand. Removing my earbuds, I strained to hear a sound as we stood at the back of the concert hall. There were no sounds, no movement on stage, yet the air felt vibrant.

Father took that moment to cast vision into my spirit. He told me the sound I carry is for joy and healing. I wasn't sure if it had to do with songwriting, music or my writing, but it didn't matter in that moment. My curiosity was brimming.

I asked Father if I could go on stage for a closer look. I wanted to explore the instruments, for there were some I didn't recognize. I saw what looked like a small hollowed-out log-shaped percussion instrument from the back of the room. He nodded in assent, and I eagerly walked forward.

Stepping onto the stage, I immediately noticed that what I thought was a cello was actually an upright bass. Although I didn't hear any music, I sensed "swell," like when a piece of music increases in intensity, power and fullness. Further back on stage were vibes, chimes, a xylophone, timpani, and two cymbals on an upright rectangular frame. As I approached the opposite corner of the stage, there were the instruments I didn't recognize. But there was no time to explore; Father wanted to take me to the next room. I didn't get a chance to touch any of those instruments, but I wasn't disappointed because we were exploring together.

Meandering through the narrow, shell-like passageways, we silently headed toward a lowered doorway without a door. It was about half the height of a household doorway. I had to stoop down to enter. As I took this posture, I understood this was the humility room. I laid on my back on a narrow strip of the white floor with small pools of clear liquid on either side of me. I asked Father if it was water, and He said it was pure. He then instructed me to dip my finger into one of the pools and put a dab of liquid on my forehead, heart and stomach.

Suddenly, my body relaxed and released the tension I hadn't known I was carrying. I felt tranquility like I had never experienced. Peace reigned here, and I rested. I don't know how long I laid there; there were no clocks, nor did I wear a watch or have my cell phone with me.

When it was time to move on, we were immediately outdoors. On the left, tall red rocks like the ones I'd seen in the Grand Canyon towered above the desert floor. The air felt comfortable, not too hot despite the midday brightness.

Anticipating my question about the purpose of this place, Father said:

"Rough edges are smoothed here."

I instinctively knew He meant rough edges in character got rubbed smooth. Refining happened in this place.

Not lingering too long outside, we went to the last location of my visit. We were indoors again, in the white seashell walled place. Ahead was a small round doorway about waist high that no one entered. Peering into the cylindrical opening to the room, I saw a red striped pattern on the walls made of something liquid, like ink. I suddenly realized that it represented Jesus' shed blood.

In the blink of an eye, Jesus stood in front of me, serving me communion. He led me through a meaningful time of remembrance of the sacrifice He made on my behalf. I've not looked at communion the same way since this experience.

After this emotionally touching moment, it was time to leave. I knew in my spirit that I'd return. I believed Father wanted to show me more.

Back in my blue recliner, I slowly opened my eyes. I had no idea how much time had passed. I marveled at what I had just experienced.

The following day, while watching a teaching video replay, Isaiah 60:5 was spoken:

"Then you will understand and be radiant. Our hearts will be thrilled and swell with joy. The fullness of the sea will flow to you, and the wealth of the nations will be transferred to you!"

When I heard the phrase "swell with joy," my spirit recognized it as part of my city visit. It was the phrase I heard while standing in the concert hall. Thank you, Lord, for dropping meaning into that shared experience with You.

Getting these glimpses into what delights Father's heart inspires me to be still and know that He is God (Psalm 46:10). I'll sit with Him for hours, and it feels like minutes. Sometimes He shows me places that delight His heart, and other times I sit near Him in a particular place we both enjoy. Even though the surroundings are spectacular, I find the most pleasure in simply being in His presence. Psalm 16:11 says:

"You will make known to me the way of life;

In Your presence is fullness of joy;

In Your right hand there are pleasures forever."

Chapter Fourteen:

All In

Without opening my eyes, my left hand instinctively reached over to my nightstand. Grabbing my notepad and pen, I opened one eye and scribbled a word hoping I'd be able to read it in the morning. Placing the pen and paper back onto the nightstand, I went back to sleep.

Hours later, with the sun shimmering through the blinds, "Here I Am to Worship" was the chorus on my heart as my eyes blinked a couple of times before opening. Were angels singing in my dream? Was I singing in my sleep? I've known that I was having a worship time in previous mornings, but I wasn't sure this time.

Surprisingly, I remembered writing the word "canopy" in the middle of the night. Looking up the definition in the Merriam-Webster Dictionary, I saw three choices for meanings. For some reason, the third one about being a transparent covering over a plane's cockpit stuck out to me. It keeps the pilot safe.

Later, when reading Proverbs 2:7-8 TPT, I understood why. "For the Lord has a hidden storehouse of wisdom made accessible to his godly ones. He becomes your personal bodyguard as you follow his ways, protecting and guarding you as you choose what is right."

What? I have my own personal bodyguard? Feeling safe is a big deal to me. Especially in this season of learning how to let my emotions coexist with my logic. I have to learn the vocabulary and figure out what to do with feelings that pop up. I feel vulnerable. I told my coach, "I feel out of control! My life feels like a whack-a-mole game!"

This same coach suggested I use colorful pens to draw what I'm feeling as a way to express my buried emotions. Rather than drawing specific pictures, she told me to practice emoting by letting the pen movements flow freely. My homework was to discover my buried feelings: acknowledge, accept, value and practice them. I told her, "It's the accepting and valuing part that is really hard."

It's been several months since I've been living in this new reality. I can tell when my emotions go into hiding, because I feel a dullness. It's as if my world loses its vibrancy. I have to be honest and admit that at first, I am not even aware it's happening. It can be several days before I clue into my diminished emotions. That probably comes from years of being good at ignoring them.

One clue that I have disconnected emotions is when I walk away feeling nothing after talking with someone. Another sign is when I'm reading the Bible and glossing over the stories, not entering into the scenes from the characters' point of view. I show up passively rather than interacting with the living and active Word of God (Hebrews 4:12).

When I finally realize what's going on, I spend time with the Lord, walking through the steps to trust Him with my feelings of disappointment, frustration or sadness. The steps include being honest with God, letting Him know how I'm feeling about what I perceive is happening. I've learned that He is a good listener, and He listens without judgment. "Therefore, there is now no condemnation for those who are in Christ

Jesus." Romans 8:10

Sometimes I'll ask God, "What do You want me to know about what's going on?" Other times, I'll ask, "Does what I believe match up with Your Word and the reality of my current situation?" Then, I ask what I should do about it, or I'll ask Him what He wants to do about it, depending on what is causing the angst.

Writing in my journal, having a two-way conversation with Him, helps me reconnect. Sometimes taking a walk and talking to God out loud helps. For now, staying connected emotionally takes focus and extra awareness. I've been relying on my learned self-protection for so long that it takes intentionality to work through the times when my heart fades into the background.

Usually, what happens at the end of working through the steps is that I surrender anew, and I thank God for what He has done.

Recently, when I was processing the emotion of disappointment, God asked me how I typically handle disappointment. I replied, "Ignore it. Bury it. Set it aside. Besides, I'm an optimist, so disappointment does not have a place in the optimist grid, or does it?"

He answered, *"Yes, it does. You can still be an optimist and face, handle and manage disappointment."*

Being the curious person I am, I asked, "How?"

"By bringing Me into the equation. You don't have to handle difficult emotions like this by yourself. Remember, I am Immanuel. I am with you. That's why Jesus said, 'I am with you, even until the end of the age.'" Matthew 28:20

My old "equation" was to first lean on my analytical ability, mental resources and ability to figure things out. Now it doesn't feel good to be disengaged or not fully present emotionally. Admittingly, I often feel uncomfortable as I'm learning and exploring the language of emotions. It's like I've entered into a whole new world.

Last month when I was traveling, I called an empathetic friend and opened the phone call with, "I'm grieving! No one has died, but my heart is feeling the loss of..." My friend listened, gave some encouraging words and later prayed. While I didn't feel better right then, I awoke the next day feeling lighter, as if God had ministered to me as I slept. Psalm 127:2 says, "He gives to His beloved even in his sleep."

God continually invites me to be with Him in my heartache, disappointment and other emotions. Here is a recent journal excerpt:

> "But now I know Jesus is interested in how I feel. I don't have to go into numbness." He completely understands my emotions as Jesus was well acquainted with suffering and pain. Isaiah 53:3

In a different journal, I wrote:

> "I believe I can trust You, God. I will trust You. I am *all in* with You.
>
> You held back nothing from me when You sent your Son to die on the cross so we could have a relationship. I certainly cannot hold back anything from You to protect myself. Besides, how do I know what's best for me anyway? I may think I know, but You formed me. You know what's best for me. Therefore, being *all in*

with You is the safest thing I can do. I TRUST YOU, LORD! Thank you, Lord!"

Chapter Fifteen:

The End Is the Beginning

"You're the wrong person for the job!" loudly paraded across the forefront of my mind as I drove home from the first night of the conference. Despite proactive planning and an assistant to help manage onsite tasks, I felt frustrated, dissatisfied, and done. Something was "off" internally.

For four years, I had put my heart and soul into helping like-minded friends put on women's conferences around the country. Tapping into my event planning background, I managed the details and did behind-the-scenes projects to make the conference run as smoothly as possible. My favorite thing to do fell under the heading of "Team Member Care." I made sure the team members were welcomed, fed, and had what they needed to carry out their portion of the weekend experience.

We enjoyed providing a beautiful setting for women to pause from their busy lives, enter into a safe space, and meet with Jesus. Meaningful worship, excellent Biblical teaching, and inspirational prayer stations were available in a peaceful environment.

Typically, the first day of the conference was when I got to see my administrative work come to life. The goal was to have the event flow seamlessly so that attendees would not be distracted from having meaningful moments with Jesus. On this particular weekend, as I oversaw the logistics outside the venue, I felt overwhelmed and agitated.

The team was twice as big as usual, and I couldn't connect with them all. There were on-the-spot decisions I needed to make without having pertinent pieces of information. I couldn't check in with the onsite vendors because too many other situations called for my immediate attention. Things were unraveling. I had no idea that this was the beginning of the end.

It turned out that the 350+ women had wonderful experiences at the conference. Their written evaluations commented on how smooth the event ran and how deeply and intimately they experienced Jesus. While I was grateful for these testimonies and encouraging comments, my emotions didn't reflect positivity.

I wrestled with the validity of the phrase, "You're the wrong person for the job." Was I just sleep-deprived, and my perspective skewed? When we had these weekend events, I usually didn't sleep well because of the sheer number of details involved. When trying to sleep, an unfinished element came to mind, so I'd make a note of it on a nearby notepad. On nights where there were too many tasks coming to mind, I'd make my way to the living room, get on my desktop computer, and work. The condition of my physical state was not new, but my inner turmoil was unexpected.

Late one night after the last day of the conference, I climbed onto our backyard trampoline, not to jump but to lay down and look up at the starry sky. I poured my heart out to God, trying to get clarity and resolve. I rehashed situations from the weekend event, evaluated my decisions and responses, considered various scenarios. They were not all negative; there were moments I was grateful for as well. I desperately needed to process the phrase that had scrolled through my mind since the first night of the event.

After telling God everything I was wrestling with, His peaceful presence came near. He didn't answer all of my questions or enter into the evaluation process that I was baiting Him into, but He gave me a sense of His heart in the situation. By the time I got up to go into the house, I knew that the phrase "You're the wrong person for the job." was not an accusation from the enemy or a reaction to my challenging experience. It was an invitation from God to enter into a new season.

I realized that God wanted me to remain in this ministry but stop coordinating the event. He wanted me to simplify and shift my focus. He wanted prayer to be my main contribution. That meant no more proactive planning meetings, managing conference details, or taking care of the team. The last part was hard to let go of because feeding the team and making sure they had what they needed to serve was my favorite thing to do the entire weekend.

Next came the task of telling my friend, whose ministry I volunteered for, that I was stepping out of my role of planning and organizing. Part of me felt awful. It wasn't like they had countless people lining up to do this particular job. But I believed God had a provision in mind for the need.

Several honest conversations, much prayer, and trust in what God had in mind for future conferences followed.

Two years later, our next women's events took place in Chiang Mai, Thailand. Uncertain about how I'd function as a Prayer Team Member without the added responsibilities of managing details, I went anticipating the new things that God would do.

I wondered if my detailed thinking would be a distraction or an opportunity to continually ask Father what was mine to do and what was not.

He exceeded my expectations! I felt free to participate in the conferences in ways I hadn't before. I enjoyed engaging with the ladies over meals. I got to pray for healing for some of the ladies, and God healed them!

Inviting the women to come forward to receive a prayer of blessing was the last thing we did at each conference. I had heard many of our prayer team ladies say that these prayer times were the highlight of their weekend. I had to be in tear-down mode before this prayer time at all of our previous events. In Thailand, I got to experience these one-on-one prayer times for the first time.

There I was, standing in front of the platform, anticipating which ladies God would send my way. My heart was beating with anticipation and gratitude. It wasn't long before three to four ladies at a time were standing in line for their turn. Seeing God touch these women with affirmations that only He could have known made me realize why our team had said they enjoyed doing this. These ladies went home feeling seen and deeply loved by Him. They encountered the One who loved them like no other.

This Thailand trip confirmed that stepping into this new season was the best decision. Because of not needing to think about keeping things on schedule and preparing for the next thing, I felt free to flow in the Holy Spirit like never before. It was a beautiful unfolding like that of a peacock's tail feathers.

During team prayer, a teammate identified the peacock's beautiful unfurling as part of my journey. Thailand was the beginning of accepting God's invitation into my new reality. For me to experience this exciting, satisfying new thing, there had to be an ending. I discovered that sometimes, the end is actually the beginning. The *more* of God is on the other side of your obedience!

Isaiah 43:19 says, "Behold. I will do something new, now it will spring forth; will you not be aware of it? I will even make a roadway in the wilderness, rivers in the desert."

Psalm 62:8 says, "Trust in Him at all times, O people; Pour out your heart before Him; God is a refuge for us. Selah."

Next Steps

After reading these chapters, you may be wondering, "Where do I go from here?" or, "What one thing can I do right now to help me grow in intimacy with God?" This heart posture will attract answers. Father is all about relationship and wants to connect with you. Realize though, there is no magic formula for intimacy with Him.

Understand, too, that because each of us is wired differently, we hear God's voice differently. Some see and hear, (as I shared in my stories), some feel and others *know*. They just have a sense of knowing what to do and when to do it. When pressed for answers as to why, they may not have a reasonable explanation; they just know.

Besides saying yes to Jesus Christ, that His death on the cross was ample payment for your sin, trusting Him with every area of your life is essential. What helps me to continually surrender is believing He is good and He loves me with an everlasting love. As a believer in Jesus Christ, you have Holy Spirit living inside of you (1 Cor. 3:16). You can grow in learning how He leads as you grow in hearing His voice.

Look at one last two-way conversation from my journal dated October 2020. God started by asking me a question.

"Why are you wanting a label for where you're at?"

"I want to know that I'm getting everything You want me to get out of this time."

"You are! You are experiencing above and beyond! You are in the more of Me that you asked for.

As you stay hungry for more, you'll go deeper and deeper into the depth of who I am. I will continue to reveal Myself to you and make My ways known to you as you spend time with Me in the Secret Place.

It's a privilege that only comes to those who sit near Me, as you've read in Psalm 25:14. It's a private place reserved for the lovers of God, and you have to choose to go there. It doesn't happen automatically.

Setting time aside and the heart space to receive my revelations are key."

From this conversation, I'm reminded that staying hungry, asking for more and sitting near Him accelerated my journey. Practically speaking, I have some current practices that I do in my times with Father. Depending on my life phase or my season, these daily practices can change.

Daily Practices:

• Listening to specific verses about my identity in Christ

• Listening to my worship playlist or grabbing my guitar and worshipping

• Reading a chapter in Proverbs

• Paying attention when verses jump off the page

For example, the topic of wisdom came up twice in Proverbs 4, and it grabbed my attention.

Proverbs 4:7 TPT, "Wisdom is the most valuable commodity-so buy it! Revelation-knowledge is what you need-so invest in it!"

Proverbs 4: 8 TPT, "Wisdom will exalt you when you exalt her truth. She will lead you to honor and favor when you live your life by her insights."

These led me to look at James 1:5, "But if any of you lacks wisdom, let him ask of God, who gives to all generously and without reproach, and it will be given to him."

Because wisdom stood out to me, I prayed about it. My prayer was:

"Grow my capacity for wisdom, Lord! And I want increasing discernment. These go hand-in-hand, don't they?"

This question led me down a road to research the difference between wisdom and discernment. As you can see, I investigate and ask questions about things that stand out while I read.

Occasional Practices:

• Reviewing notes and verse references from past Bible Study courses or books

• Comparing verses in various Bible translations for deeper understanding. I like NASB, AMP and TPT.

Simply Come Near

In reading stories of how God spoke to me, your heart and mind have expanded in awareness of Holy Spirit. You could start with a simple question as I did:

"Holy Spirit, who are You?"

Then, be willing to say yes whenever you feel Holy Spirit prompting you to do something. Your hearing will improve and boldness will increase as you practice. Doing a word study on Holy Spirit in your preferred Bible translation will also give you courage.

I don't want you to think it's "a + b = c." There is no formula for encountering God. Just like I am excited when our grown children come home to spend time with me, Father is thrilled when His children want to be with Him. I'd say it's more of a heart posture turned toward Him that matters most.

In your journey, Father is saying, "I'm proud of you!" and continually inviting you to simply come near. You are beloved.

"There is a private place reserved for the lovers of God where they sit near Him and receive the revelation-secrets of His promises." Psalm 25:14 TPT

If you'd like to receive a free PDF of chapter questions for *Journey Into More*, please go to:

www.journeyintomore.com

About the Author

Sandi Sadako is a home coffee roaster, writer, intercessor, speaker, blogger, worship leader, and avid traveler who's been to 49 states and 16 countries. Anyplace near water, especially the ocean, is Sandi's favorite getaway spot. However, Sandi's favorite place to be is in the presence of her Father, partnering with Him wherever He leads. Journey with this wife, mom of three and mixed terrier owner as she experiences God in conversations, missionary trips, her blue recliner and her intimate journal pages. Sandi's calm, joyful presence will lead you to engage with God in meaningful ways.

Be inspired to go from believer to beloved!

In addition to speaking from her varied life experiences and Holy Spirit-led adventures, facilitating Immanuel prayer is the delight of Sandi's heart. The purpose of Immanuel prayer is greater intimacy with Jesus, experiencing His interactive presence, and realizing that He enjoys being with you.

Contact Sandi for your next gathering: sandisadako@earthlink.net

Follow Sandi on Facebook, Instagram, Tik Tok and YouTube: @sandisadako

Subscribe to Sandi's blog: www.sandisadako.com

Learn more about Sandi's *believer to beloved* trainings: www.heargodsimply.com

With help from

Made in the USA
Coppell, TX
12 July 2022

79885730R00066